Grateful in Love

This journal belongs to

and

Introduction

Most people think of gratitude as simply feeling grateful. Gratitude in action actually has two components: "the quality of being thankful" (Oxford English Dictionary) that most people associate with the term and, crucially, a demonstrated appreciation of what's been done to merit that thankfulness. In other words, feelings of gratitude must manifest into actions of gratitude.

Consider this example: Let's say that you feel grateful for your vehicle. It gets you to work, helps you see friends and loved ones, lets you go on trips and excursions, and so on. But are you really grateful for your car if you neglect to get it oil changes or other regular maintenance? Sooner rather than later, your car will sputter out, and your *feeling* of gratitude for it won't have mattered much because it didn't translate into the appropriate action of *expressing* gratitude.

Relationships with others, especially your partner, need to be similarly maintained. Your *feelings* of gratitude must be accompanied by *actions* of gratitude. If not, your relationships may sputter out too. Grateful people don't simply feel thankful; they *act* thankful.

Implementing the feelings and actions of gratitude into your life as a practice can have a profound effect on happiness. One 2011 study published in *Emotion* reveals that "gratitude is strongly related to well-being" and that this greatly influences a person's health, coping ability, and relationships. These individuals are happier, can appreciate the little things more, handle stress better, and have stronger intimate relationships.

Beginning a practice of gratitude with your partner can help you actively see each other more positively. A 2010 study published in *Clinical Psychology Review* found that couples that expressed gratitude for one another had a "more positive perception" of their partner and were thus better able to "express . . . [their] relationship concerns," which improved their communication and relationships overall.

As a Certified Relationship Coach, I've guided hundreds of clients to happier and healthier relationships. Through my practice and life, I've discovered that one of the most powerful (and easiest) ways to have the kind of happy relationship we all want is by enjoying a regular practice of gratitude. My husband and I have both been married before. We understood too well how much bitter and petty resentments can wear down a relationship. It was our decision to cultivate a practice of gratitude together not only to improve our own lives but also to ensure that we remain grateful and in love together. This book offers you the same opportunity. The gratitude practice you'll find here will not only encourage you and your partner to learn new things about each other, but it will also help you and your partner have the kind of supportive and caring relationship you've always hoped for.

How to Use This Journal

This gratitude journal is for you and your partner to complete together.

What does *partner* mean for the purposes of this journal? That's up to you. Anyone can be your partner as long as you choose to engage with them in this gratitude journal. Your partner is likely a spouse, new or long-term sweetheart, or fiancé, but it could also be a close friend, roommate, family member, colleague, co-parent, or "situation-ship."

This book is composed of over 200 Guided Prompts, Gratitude Lists, and All about Your Partner Prompts. Each component of this book is followed by two sets of lines, so both you and your partner will have space to write out your own unique responses. As a starting point, this journal will give you an opportunity to share regular quality time with your partner. It will elicit great conversations and, with some effort, improve your communication.

The Guided Prompts encourage you to think about positive (and even negative) aspects of your life in order to feel more grateful. You can answer in just a couple of sentences. The purpose is not to write an essay, but rather to jot down some ideas and then discuss what you've written in greater detail with your partner.

The Gratitude Lists are a wonderful practice you can employ in your daily life and will ideally become a habit. You can share these lists with your partner, and you will almost certainly discover new things about yourselves and what you're grateful for in the process.

The All about Your Partner Prompts are geared toward helping you feel more positive, loving, and appreciative of this special person with whom you've chosen to work through this journal. These prompts will give you an opportunity to think about what you most admire about your partner.

Gratitude is best cultivated through regular practice, so figure out what works best for you and your partner. You might answer one prompt a day over coffee or choose to do so once a week. You can also spend some time while on a date, road trip, regular phone call, or vacation. The most important thing is that you are connecting with one another. Feeling and practicing an attitude of gratitude has been connected to a happier overall life, so it's time you both get started. Best of luck on what will be a fun and fulfilling adventure together.

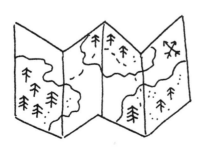

{ Write a thank-you note to your partner that includes at least one specific thing that they have done that you're thankful for, and then highlight how what they did helped you.

_____

_____

_____

_____

_____

_____

_____

{ Both the giver and the receiver reap the benefits of gratitude. Write about a time your partner expressed their gratitude for you and how it made you feel.

_____

_____

_____

_____

_____

_____

_____

1

{ Sometimes a gratitude practice needs to start small because it can be a struggle to change your mindset. What's one little thing you feel grateful for on a daily basis?

_____

_____

_____

_____

_____

_____

_____

{ What does gratitude mean to you? How do you show you are grateful? How does it make you feel? What do you like about feeling grateful?

_____

_____

_____

_____

_____

_____

_____

What does being thankful mean to you? How do you show you are thankful? Is it different for you from showing gratitude? Why or why not?

What is an accomplishment you're proud of? What are some steps you had to take to achieve that accomplishment? Was it difficult? Why or why not?

3

What is a way that your partner has helped you? Did they take up the slack in some way or encourage/support you in a goal?

What is something your partner has done that has made you feel appreciated? Can you elaborate on that feeling?

List 10 things you would have never been able to do without your partner's support and help—for example, going back to school, getting another job, and so on.

1. _____
2. _____
3. _____
4. _____
5. _____
6. _____
7. _____
8. _____
9. _____
10. _____

1. _____
2. _____
3. _____
4. _____
5. _____
6. _____
7. _____
8. _____
9. _____
10. _____

Write about the tasks your partner does around the house. Are they things you would not want to do? Has this made life easier for you?

{ Write about something that took effort for you to learn. Why did you keep at it despite the difficulty? What did you learn from the experience?

{ Write about a quality that you admire in others that you don't feel you have yourself. Is it something you could cultivate in yourself more? How?

What made you decide to pursue your line of work or whatever occupies your time each day? Is it what you'd like to be doing, or is it a stepping-stone to something greater?

We feel fully loved when we feel comfortable to be ourselves without fear of judgment. In what ways does your partner show this love for you?

{ Write about something that always puts a smile on your face, whether it be your partner, a favorite pet, or a fond memory from your childhood.

{ What are some specific things about your childhood, your upbringing, where you grew up, or the people who surrounded you that you are most thankful for today?

{ Think about a recent success you've had or a goal you've
reached. Is there anyone who helped you achieve it? What
would you say to thank them?

_____

_____

_____

_____

_____

_____

_____

_____

{ What are four things you do really well? Now write about
four things your partner does really well. How do your lists
complement one another?

_____

_____

_____

_____

_____

_____

_____

_____

List 10 times your partner surprised you with something—for instance, unexpected gifts, times they took on a task or chore for you, a nice note they wrote you, and so on.

1. _____
2. _____
3. _____
4. _____
5. _____
6. _____
7. _____
8. _____
9. _____
10. _____

1. _____
2. _____
3. _____
4. _____
5. _____
6. _____
7. _____
8. _____
9. _____
10. _____

Write about the qualities you most admire in your partner. Is your partner patient, spontaneous, funny, smart, honest, intelligent, levelheaded, respectful, or something else entirely?

Think about the last time you disappointed yourself. What was it? How did you not reach the mark? How can you still feel thankful for the experience?

When you think about that time you disappointed yourself, in what ways could you do better next time? Is there anything positive that may have come from the experience?

13

{ List three people who annoy you. What do you most dislike about them? Can you think of positive traits they might have? Write those down too.

_____

_____

_____

_____

_____

_____

_____

{ We often dislike traits in others that we also dislike in ourselves. How does knowing that help you feel more compassion for them and for yourself?

_____

_____

_____

_____

_____

_____

_____

Write out a list of your stressors. Can you change anything about them? If not, is there a way you can change your perspective about them?

What is something you hoped you'd get but didn't? Did something happen later that showed it was for the best that you didn't get it?

{ Write a note to your partner about a time when they impressed you. What was it? How did it inform how you feel about them today?

_____

_____

_____

_____

_____

_____

_____

{ People come into our lives for a reason, season, or lifetime. Who has taught you something important? What would you say to thank them?

_____

_____

_____

_____

_____

_____

_____

List 10 people who make your life better on a regular basis. Consider your partner, friends, family members, or coworkers or maybe even your favorite barista.

1. _____
2. _____
3. _____
4. _____
5. _____
6. _____
7. _____
8. _____
9. _____
10. _____

1. _____
2. _____
3. _____
4. _____
5. _____
6. _____
7. _____
8. _____
9. _____
10. _____

Describe the first time you met your partner. What did you think when you first saw them? Was it an immediate attraction or a more gradual one?

{ What are things that your partner does that show you they love you? Let them know if you'd like them to keep doing these things.

_____

_____

_____

_____

_____

_____

_____

{ What are things you wish your partner did to show their love for you? Have you ever told them before? Could you let them know now?

_____

_____

_____

_____

_____

_____

_____

{ Write about a time you were pleasantly surprised, whether it was a sweet message, an unexpected gift, or a kind act. What about it did you like the most?

_____

_____

_____

_____

_____

_____

_____

{ When is the last time you and your partner laughed together? What do you love most about laughing with them?

_____

_____

_____

_____

_____

_____

_____

Think about your favorite day with your partner. What happened on that day? What about it made it special? Describe what you most loved about it.

_____

_____

_____

_____

_____

_____

_____

_____

_____

Home can either be a physical place, a feeling, or a person. What does "home" mean to you? How do you know you feel "at home"?

_____

_____

_____

_____

_____

_____

_____

_____

{ What's a part of your daily life that you most dislike (a task at work, an obligation, etc.)? What is one way you could make it more enjoyable?

{ What are three positive adjectives you would use to describe yourself? Would others use those same adjectives to describe you? Why or why not?

What are 10 things you absolutely love about yourself, your personality, and/or your way of being in the world? Think about your persistence, empathy, sense of humor, and so on.

1. _____
2. _____
3. _____
4. _____
5. _____
6. _____
7. _____
8. _____
9. _____
10. _____

- -

1. _____
2. _____
3. _____
4. _____
5. _____
6. _____
7. _____
8. _____
9. _____
10. _____

Part of loving someone involves accepting them alongside their imperfections. Write about what you perceive to be your partner's worst traits and why you love them anyway.

{ What are three positive adjectives you would use to describe
your partner? Do they know that you think those things
about them? If not, tell them.

_____

_____

_____

_____

_____

_____

_____

_____

{ Describe what you most like about what you do on a daily
basis, whether it's your job or something else. If you struggle
to think of something positive, think harder.

_____

_____

_____

_____

_____

_____

_____

_____

Who was your favorite person growing up? A parent, sibling, special friend, or teacher? What traits or behaviors did you most appreciate about them?

What's something you're looking forward to (vacation, promotion, eating pizza for dinner, etc.)? How can you bring the joy you feel about that future something into the present?

{ Describe something physical that you enjoy (dancing, hugging, etc.). Does it make your life easier? Does it remind you of happy times or a special someone?

{ What do you most appreciate about your body? How has it served you as you've moved through life? How is it strong, beautiful, amazing, or impressive?

{ What do other people seem to like about you? What kind of compliments do you receive often? If you're unsure, ask your partner or a friend.

_____

_____

_____

_____

_____

_____

_____

{ What is your favorite part about what you do every day? What does your daily routine or job allow you to do that you couldn't do if you were doing something else?

_____

_____

_____

_____

_____

_____

_____

What are 10 things that make you feel the most loved when
someone does them for you? Think about gifts, public displays
of affection, compliments, listening, and so on.

1. _____

2. _____

3. _____

4. _____

5. _____

6. _____

7. _____

8. _____

9. _____

10. _____

- -

1. _____

2. _____

3. _____

4. _____

5. _____

6. _____

7. _____

8. _____

9. _____

10. _____

What one behavior would you change about your partner? If you could actually change it, would you choose to? Explain why or why not.

{ What's something (a hobby, activity, etc.) you loved to do as a child? What did you love most about it? How did it make you feel?

_____

_____

_____

_____

_____

_____

_____

_____

{ Do you still do that something today? If not, is there a way you could start? Think of a specific step you could take to start.

_____

_____

_____

_____

_____

_____

_____

{ Name an item that you cherish. Why is it special? What does it remind you of? Where do you keep it? When do you look at it?

_____

_____

_____

_____

_____

_____

_____

{ What are your guilty pleasures? Why do you consider them "guilty"? When do you get to do them? What do you enjoy most about them?

_____

_____

_____

_____

_____

_____

_____

{ Who is a favorite person (other than your partner) who you have in your life today? Do they have similar traits/behaviors to the favorite person you knew growing up?

_____

_____

_____

_____

_____

_____

_____

{ What is a happy memory from your childhood? It could be a single memory (like a special trip) or a recurring one (like a certain holiday).

_____

_____

_____

_____

_____

_____

_____

{ Write about something or someone you know you take for granted or often fail to appreciate because you're so used to them.

_____

_____

_____

_____

_____

_____

_____

_____

{ What's a way you could show appreciation for that something or someone today? It doesn't have to be something big. It could just be saying thanks.

_____

_____

_____

_____

_____

_____

_____

_____

What are 10 inanimate things that make your life easier or more enjoyable? For instance, consider a bag or purse, memberships or subscriptions, coffee, or glasses.

1. _____
2. _____
3. _____
4. _____
5. _____
6. _____
7. _____
8. _____
9. _____
10. _____

1. _____
2. _____
3. _____
4. _____
5. _____
6. _____
7. _____
8. _____
9. _____
10. _____

Describe your favorite memory of your partner. What about it makes it stand out the most from all your other memories?

{ What's something you love doing, but you know you don't do it often enough? It could be a hobby or activity, traveling to a specific place, or visiting someone you care about.

{ How could you start doing that something more often or regularly? Is there something you could *stop* doing to be able to have time for it?

{ What's the best compliment you've ever received from someone? Who said it to you, and why was it meaningful? Do you believe it about yourself today?

_____

_____

_____

_____

_____

_____

{ Where could you put that compliment so you might see it every day? Maybe on a sticky note next to a light switch or as a repeated calendar item on your phone?

_____

_____

_____

_____

_____

_____

_____

{ Why do you think it's important to practice gratitude? What does "practice" mean to you? What difference do you think it will make in your life?

_____

_____

_____

_____

_____

_____

_____

_____

{ Before starting this journal, how often do you feel you practiced being thankful? Regularly? Sporadically? Rarely? Were there times in the past when it was more common?

_____

_____

_____

_____

_____

_____

_____

{ Write about a time in your life that was particularly difficult but ended up leading to something better. What was the "purpose" you learned later?

_____

_____

_____

_____

_____

_____

_____

{ When was the last time you experienced an unexpected act of kindness? It can be small. How did it make your day easier? How did you feel?

_____

_____

_____

_____

_____

_____

_____

_____

What are 10 ways you could start expressing your gratitude today? Consider both personal ways (with the people in your life) and outward ways (volunteering, etc.).

1. _____
2. _____
3. _____
4. _____
5. _____
6. _____
7. _____
8. _____
9. _____
10. _____

1. _____
2. _____
3. _____
4. _____
5. _____
6. _____
7. _____
8. _____
9. _____
10. _____

If a stranger asked about your partner, how would you describe them in 10 words or fewer? How would you distill them into such a brief summary?

{ Has being thankful been difficult for you to practice? If so, why do you think that is? How has not expressing gratitude affected you?

_____

_____

_____

_____

_____

_____

_____

_____

{ Since you have started a practice of gratitude, how do you think you'll work through those difficult times in the future? Can you be grateful even when it is difficult?

_____

_____

_____

_____

_____

_____

_____

What is your favorite thing about your family? "Family" can mean your relatives, but it also means people you choose to have in your life.

What is your favorite way to relax? Is it an activity or going to a certain place? Do you feel you get to do it enough?

Is there something you do currently that doesn't contribute to your overall happiness? What is it? What would you have time for if you stopped it?

What's a step you could take to stop doing that one thing? Make it small but manageable. If it doesn't improve your life, why do it?

Write about a tiny victory you're really proud of. Why was it a victory for you? How did it make you feel to accomplish it?

_____

_____

_____

_____

_____

_____

_____

_____

What's a tradition you and your partner or you and your family/friends have that you enjoy? Is it a long-standing tradition? Did you create it together?

_____

_____

_____

_____

_____

_____

_____

_____

What are 10 things you love about where you live? Think specifically about your home, as well as broadly, like your country. What makes them special? What makes you proud to live there?

1. _____

2. _____

3. _____

4. _____

5. _____

6. _____

7. _____

8. _____

9. _____

10. _____

- -

1. _____

2. _____

3. _____

4. _____

5. _____

6. _____

7. _____

8. _____

9. _____

10. _____

What do you envision as an ideal future for your partner? What would be their job? Where would they live? What would they do on a normal day?

Do you have a favorite article of clothing? Why is it your favorite? When is the last time you wore it?

What's something beautiful you drive or walk past every day? If you can't think of anything, take some time to look around the next time you're out.

{ What's a secret talent you have? Do the people close to you
know this "secret"? If so, why or why not? Could you let
them know?

_____

_____

_____

_____

_____

_____

_____

_____

{ What are the things you turn to when you need comfort? A
special meal? A blanket or certain outfit? A beloved movie?
What about these items helps you find solace?

_____

_____

_____

_____

_____

_____

_____

_____

List 10 things you like about your job, whether you work in or out of the home. Think about people you work with, your job's purpose, some tasks you enjoy, and so on.

1. _____

2. _____

3. _____

4. _____

5. _____

6. _____

7. _____

8. _____

9. _____

10. _____

- -

1. _____

2. _____

3. _____

4. _____

5. _____

6. _____

7. _____

8. _____

9. _____

10. _____

What do you think/know makes your partner happy? It could be cuddling, a specific movie, eating at a new restaurant, or spring weather.

Write about one of your role models. Who are they? What is something that they taught you, and how have you used it in your life?

_____

_____

_____

_____

_____

_____

_____

Write a thank-you note to that role model. What did they do that you appreciated? In what ways did they influence you? Let them know.

_____

_____

_____

_____

_____

_____

_____

{ What's a quotation (from a book or a movie or elsewhere) that has inspired you? Look it up and write it down here. Give context if that's helpful.

_____

_____

_____

_____

_____

_____

_____

{ Why did that particular quote resonate with you? What do you feel it says about you, your beliefs, or what you hope for yourself or for the future?

_____

_____

_____

_____

_____

_____

_____

Write a quick thank-you to your body. In what ways has it helped you? What does it allow you to do on a daily basis?

What's something small you enjoy every morning? It could be getting that first cup of coffee, running a hot shower, or the quiet before the chaos.

What's something small you enjoy every night? It could be getting between the bedsheets, watching TV, or having a phone call with a loved one.

When is the last time you saw something truly beautiful? What was it? What about it struck you? How did it make you feel?

List your 10 favorite things about the season you're *currently* in. For example, carving pumpkins, sipping cold drinks outside, throwing snowballs, watching fireworks, or blooming flowers.

1. _____
2. _____
3. _____
4. _____
5. _____
6. _____
7. _____
8. _____
9. _____
10. _____

- - - - - - - - - - - - - - - - - - - -

1. _____
2. _____
3. _____
4. _____
5. _____
6. _____
7. _____
8. _____
9. _____
10. _____

What makes your partner *un*happy? It could be traffic, a specific person, or a certain chore. Is there a way you could help them in this area?

{ What is something positive you did recently for a stranger? It could be anything from holding a door open for someone to paying them a compliment.

_____

_____

_____

_____

_____

_____

_____

{ How did it make you feel when you did that something good? Did you like how it felt? Is it something you would want to continue?

_____

_____

_____

_____

_____

_____

_____

_____

{ Do you share positive things you see with your partner? How
could you start telling them about joyful things in your life in
a more deliberate way?

_____

_____

_____

_____

_____

_____

_____

{ Write about a recent purchase that has made your life easier. It
could be something as small as a new travel coffee mug.

_____

_____

_____

_____

_____

_____

_____

{ Write about your favorite toy (from childhood) or pet (then or now). What about it/them did you most like and appreciate? How did it/they make your life better?

_____

_____

_____

_____

_____

_____

_____

_____

{ Who was the last person to make you smile? A stranger? A sweetheart? What did they do that made you smile? Did it help make your day better?

_____

_____

_____

_____

_____

_____

_____

_____

{ What is your favorite way to feel cared for? Fresh haircut?
Clean bedsheets? Can you make time to care for yourself in
the next 24 hours?

_____

_____

_____

_____

_____

_____

_____

_____

{ How is your life more positive and joyful today than it was a
year ago? What are the major things that have contributed to
those changes?

_____

_____

_____

_____

_____

_____

_____

_____

_____

List 10 things that always make you smile, such as funny movies or books, jokes, comedians you like, or something goofy your pet does.

1. _____
2. _____
3. _____
4. _____
5. _____
6. _____
7. _____
8. _____
9. _____
10. _____

- -

1. _____
2. _____
3. _____
4. _____
5. _____
6. _____
7. _____
8. _____
9. _____
10. _____

Is there a pet peeve that you find difficult to accept in your partner? How can you work to overlook it or learn to appreciate it?

{ Pick one thing that's made you joyful recently and write a thank-you to someone involved. "Thank you _____ for encouraging me to seek a new job . . ."

{ Write about a recent experience you had of being out in nature. Where were you? What were you doing? What did you see that you liked?

{ Do you like being out in nature? Is there a particular spot that's your favorite? Can you make plans with someone special to go there soon?

_____

_____

_____

_____

_____

_____

{ What's your favorite part of what you consider to be your job? Camaraderie with coworkers? A certain task? Your job's mission? How could you enjoy it more?

_____

_____

_____

_____

_____

_____

{ What's your least favorite part of your job? Is there a way you could make it enjoyable? Be creative; there can always be a silver lining.

{ What is your favorite time of year? It could be a season or a time around a certain holiday. What about it always makes you happy?

{ What are three ways you can *act* grateful? Gratitude should entail more than just feeling thankful, but these acts don't have to be big or elaborate.

{ Do you think you show your thanks *enough* on a daily basis, or is there a chance you should show it more? Why or why not?

List 10 groups or places where you feel like you "belong." Think about places of worship, organizations, and community groups. Brainstorm ideas of places or groups you could join.

1. _____

2. _____

3. _____

4. _____

5. _____

6. _____

7. _____

8. _____

9. _____

10. _____

- -

1. _____

2. _____

3. _____

4. _____

5. _____

6. _____

7. _____

8. _____

9. _____

10. _____

Can you think of a time or times that you were hard on your partner? What are ways you could focus on your gratitude for them
in order to practice more patience and compassion instead?

Theodore Roosevelt said, "Comparison is the thief of joy." Have you been comparing yourself lately? How did comparing yourself actually hamper your ability to feel grateful?

What would it be like if you didn't compare yourself? If you weren't better or worse than anyone? Can you be okay just as you are?

{ Name a song that always makes you feel more grateful after you hear it. Why does it make you feel that way? Can you listen to it soon?

{ Are there ways you're harder on yourself than on others? What are they? Do you consider the messages you tell yourself to be kind or mean?

Would you speak to a friend the way you speak to yourself? Why or why not? Could you speak to yourself like you were your own "friend"?

_____

_____

_____

_____

_____

_____

_____

_____

What ways could you practice more compassion with yourself? Consider what you would suggest a friend do in the same situation.

_____

_____

_____

_____

_____

_____

_____

_____

{ What does being a "good friend" mean to you? Are you a
good friend? How does being a good friend make you feel
more thankful for your relationships?

_____

_____

_____

_____

_____

_____

_____

{ What do you want from friendships in your life? Do you have
friends in your life today who give you those things? Why or
why not?

_____

_____

_____

_____

_____

_____

_____

_____

We feel more grateful for what we have when we create. List 10 ways you are or could be creative. Consider gardening, making a household organizational chart, or taking photos.

1. _____
2. _____
3. _____
4. _____
5. _____
6. _____
7. _____
8. _____
9. _____
10. _____

1. _____
2. _____
3. _____
4. _____
5. _____
6. _____
7. _____
8. _____
9. _____
10. _____

What's something you often think about your partner but don't usually say out loud? Maybe it's "Thank you" or "I love your laugh." Say it now.

Are there community groups or social organizations you're a part of? What do you like about them? If not, which ones would you like to join?

_____

_____

_____

_____

_____

_____

_____

How often do you tell your family members that you appreciate them? What actions could you take to start doing this regularly? It could be as simple as writing a note or a text.

_____

_____

_____

_____

_____

_____

_____

_____

{ How do you feel about your relationship with your parents
or the people who raised you? Are you currently the kind of
offspring you'd like to be? Are there ways you could improve?

{ Do you have a "family of choice" (people who may not
be blood relations)? Who are they? How do they feel like
family to you?

{ How do you handle being sad? How does giving yourself
opportunities for sadness allow you to feel more thankful for
the times when you're happy?

{ What were you like as a teenager? Were you very different
than the way you are now? In what ways are you still like your
younger self?

Write a note to your teenage self. What did they do best? What could you thank them for? What would you want to let them know?

What things did you like to do as a teenager? Are they things you still do now or things you would possibly like to do now?

List 10 things that you do or could do daily to make each day the best it could be. Think about connecting with a friend, listening to a certain podcast, and so on.

1. _____
2. _____
3. _____
4. _____
5. _____
6. _____
7. _____
8. _____
9. _____
10. _____

- - - - - - - - - - - - - - - - - - - -

1. _____
2. _____
3. _____
4. _____
5. _____
6. _____
7. _____
8. _____
9. _____
10. _____

What is your partner's biggest accomplishment in life so far? A job promotion? Running a marathon? How did they accomplish it? What's their next goal?

How do you handle conflict? Do you fight, flee, or freeze? In what ways have your conflict strategies helped you navigate difficult situations in the past?

What are the ways you are thankful for how you handle conflicts? What steps do you take to ensure that you handle disagreeing in a respectful manner?

{ When you and your partner have a disagreement, how do you
reengage with them? How could practicing gratitude help
you reconnect with them more easily?

_____

_____

_____

_____

_____

_____

_____

_____

{ While disagreements can be painful, they often help us learn
something new or move forward. Write a thank-you to your
partner for your last disagreement.

_____

_____

_____

_____

_____

_____

_____

_____

How do you feel about money? Does it make you feel inse-
cure, scared, grateful when you have it, or obsessed with
scarcity? Or do you find yourself taking it for granted?

What are ways that money helps improve your life? Do you
also practice donating? This could be giving of your time or
money to others.

Do your spending habits align with what you care about and most value? If not, how could you change some of your spending so they do?

If money didn't matter, how would your life look different today? Where would you live? What would you do? With whom would you spend your time?

List 10 things you'd like to *add* to your life. It could be something like connecting more frequently with loved ones or dedicating time to a hobby.

1. _____
2. _____
3. _____
4. _____
5. _____
6. _____
7. _____
8. _____
9. _____
10. _____

- -

1. _____
2. _____
3. _____
4. _____
5. _____
6. _____
7. _____
8. _____
9. _____
10. _____

Does your partner prefer to be a wallflower or the life of the party? How does their natural introversion/extroversion complement yours? How do you appreciate them for it?

{ Are there certain ways you can change your life to be more like your vision from page 86? Are there steps you could take to make it happen?

{ Where did you go on your last vacation? Whether it was a far-flung destination, a day trip, or even a staycation, what was great or fun about it? Would you like to do it again?

{ What is something you like to do that you know is silly, like
impromptu dance parties, singing in the shower, and so on?
When is the last time you did it?

{ Write about when you last took time to be silent. No reading,
watching TV, playing on your phone, or listening to the radio,
just silence.

Do you enjoy silence, or do you feel yourself needing to break it? Why? What would it be like to just *be* instead of *do*?

_____

_____

_____

_____

_____

_____

_____

_____

Estimate how many times a day you think a negative thought. Do certain things or situations bring up more negative thoughts for you?

_____

_____

_____

_____

_____

_____

_____

{ What are some positive things you could tell yourself to
counter those negative thoughts? Try using phrases like "I'm
trying . . ." or "This is an opportunity to . . ."

_____

_____

_____

_____

_____

_____

_____

{ What is a habit you could pair with the practice of gratitude?
For example, maybe thinking of things for which you feel
grateful while you're brushing your teeth each morning.

_____

_____

_____

_____

_____

_____

_____

_____

List 10 things you'd like to *subtract* from your life. Think of the things that detract from your ability to pursue other things, like having your phone by your side 24/7.

1. _____
2. _____
3. _____
4. _____
5. _____
6. _____
7. _____
8. _____
9. _____
10. _____

- - - - - - - - - - - - - - - - - - - -

1. _____
2. _____
3. _____
4. _____
5. _____
6. _____
7. _____
8. _____
9. _____
10. _____

What have you learned about yourself since you met your partner? How have you grown? How are you thankful for your partner's influence on your life?

{ What are things you appreciate in your local community or neighborhood—a nice walking trail, friendly neighbors, or a beautiful view?

_____

_____

_____

_____

_____

_____

_____

_____

{ What are some ways people help each other in your community? What are ways you could help out more? It could be as small as picking up trash as you walk your dog.

_____

_____

_____

_____

_____

_____

_____

_____

{ What's something you have today that you did not have growing up? It could be technology, a skill or talent, material items, or a character trait.

{ How could you begin your day with gratitude? It could be something as small as thinking of one positive thing before your feet hit the floor.

{ How do you prefer to spend your time? With whom would you prefer to spend time? How could you spend your time more intentionally?

_____

_____

_____

_____

_____

_____

_____

{ Gratitude must be about enjoying what you have now instead of constantly trying to cultivate what you don't have. What do you have that you love?

_____

_____

_____

_____

_____

_____

_____

{ What are services in your community that you appreciate
and that benefit you? Consider firefighters, public parks and
recreation centers, libraries, and city events.

_____

_____

_____

_____

_____

_____

_____

{ How well do you sleep at night? Do you try to sleep the
recommended seven to eight hours? What specific things
prevent you from sleeping better?

_____

_____

_____

_____

_____

_____

_____

List 10 things you like about being in a relationship with your partner. Consider shared interests, having a plus-one for events, a great listening ear, and so on.

1. _____

2. _____

3. _____

4. _____

5. _____

6. _____

7. _____

8. _____

9. _____

10. _____

- -

1. _____

2. _____

3. _____

4. _____

5. _____

6. _____

7. _____

8. _____

9. _____

10. _____

What are the things your friends and family like most about your partner and your relationship? Consider everything, including character traits, acts of kindness, how you joke together, and so on.

How do you think you would sleep if you took some time right before bed to write about what you're grateful for?

_____

_____

_____

_____

_____

_____

_____

_____

Perfect can mean "having all the required or desirable elements, qualities, or characteristics; as good as it is possible." How does that definition help you feel grateful for something you may not have been grateful for before?

_____

_____

_____

_____

_____

_____

_____

_____

What about your life now is perfect, meaning you wouldn't change one thing about it whatsoever? Write about how you're thankful for it as it is.

What is your favorite holiday? Does your family have specific traditions or rituals around the holiday that you always do to celebrate it? What are they?

{ What privileges were you born with? What privileges do you have due to your family, job, upbringing, financial status, physical abilities, and so on?

_____

_____

_____

_____

_____

_____

_____

_____

{ What do you have in your country that people in others don't? For instance, freedoms, protections, modern conveniences, educational opportunities, career options, and so on.

_____

_____

_____

_____

_____

_____

_____

_____

{ What are comforts you have that not everyone else has?
Think about air-conditioning/heating, running water, access
to food, a roof over your head, a car, and so on.

_____

_____

_____

_____

_____

_____

_____

{ Are you a morning or night person? What do you love about
that time of day? Do you have rituals that go with your favorite time?

_____

_____

_____

_____

_____

_____

_____

_____

List 10 special things your partner has done just for you, like planning a surprise for your birthday or making you your favorite meal.

1. _____
2. _____
3. _____
4. _____
5. _____
6. _____
7. _____
8. _____
9. _____
10. _____

- -

1. _____
2. _____
3. _____
4. _____
5. _____
6. _____
7. _____
8. _____
9. _____
10. _____

What are things *you* like about your partner that maybe others don't like as much? For example, consider their sarcasm, perfectionism, how they nerd out, and so on.

{ Name a book that uplifts you. What about it inspires you, makes you feel better about life, or encourages you? How often do you read it?

_____

_____

_____

_____

_____

_____

_____

{ What songs make you feel happy? Write down several. Maybe even make a playlist that you could listen to when you need a pick-me-up.

_____

_____

_____

_____

_____

_____

_____

{ What movies inspire you or give you a warm, fuzzy feeling? Is there a common theme among them? Are they all romantic comedies or underdog stories?

_____

_____

_____

_____

_____

_____

_____

{ Are there podcasts or audiobooks you listen to that give you new ideas, teach you interesting things, help you practice thankfulness, or otherwise inspire you?

_____

_____

_____

_____

_____

_____

_____

_____

When you're going through a tough time, it can be helpful to turn to something uplifting. What will you read, watch, or listen to next time you need to smile?

_____

_____

_____

_____

_____

_____

_____

What do you most like about your spiritual relationship, whether it be a higher power, the universe, spending time in the beauty of nature, or something else.

_____

_____

_____

_____

_____

_____

_____

{ Is your spiritual relationship important to you? How do you develop or cultivate it? Do you have a regular practice? If not, would you like to?

_____

_____

_____

_____

_____

_____

_____

_____

{ What technology do you use regularly? How is it helpful? Is there a way you could use it more intentionally to improve your happiness or thankfulness?

_____

_____

_____

_____

_____

_____

_____

_____

List 10 of your favorite food items. What do you like about them? Can you think about ways to bring them into your life more frequently?

1. _____
2. _____
3. _____
4. _____
5. _____
6. _____
7. _____
8. _____
9. _____
10. _____

- -

1. _____
2. _____
3. _____
4. _____
5. _____
6. _____
7. _____
8. _____
9. _____
10. _____

What are some things that you think your partner has been doing well, either in or outside your relationship? Consider things like handling a difficult situation. Have you let them know?

{ If you were to leave everyone you encounter with a gift, what would it be? Perhaps it's a smile, a compliment, or a simple thanks.

_____

_____

_____

_____

_____

_____

_____

_____

{ What's something in your future that you have to look forward to? A date night, holiday, long weekend, vacation, or event?

_____

_____

_____

_____

_____

_____

_____

_____

{ In what ways are you physically healthy? Even if your health isn't perfect, in what ways does your body help, serve, and protect you?

_____

_____

_____

_____

_____

_____

_____

_____

{ What about your physical health are you grateful for? What can you do that maybe others cannot do?

_____

_____

_____

_____

_____

_____

_____

_____

{ In what ways do you currently try to be healthy? Do you exercise? Eat well? If not, what are ways you could try to be healthier? Do you want to make this effort?

_____

_____

_____

_____

_____

_____

{ In what ways are you mentally healthy? Even if your mental health isn't perfect, you still likely have areas that are going well or that you are working on improving.

_____

_____

_____

_____

_____

_____

{ What is something that you went through recently that would have been difficult for you in the past? Write about a recent mental or emotional triumph.

_____

_____

_____

_____

_____

_____

_____

{ In what ways do you currently try to be mentally/emotionally healthy? (Note: This gratitude journal is one.) Do you meditate? Attend therapy? Spend time in nature?

_____

_____

_____

_____

_____

_____

_____

_____

List 10 hopes you have for practicing gratitude in your life.
These could be for yourself, your future, your relationships,
improved attitudes or perceptions, and so on.

1. _____

2. _____

3. _____

4. _____

5. _____

6. _____

7. _____

8. _____

9. _____

10. _____

- -

1. _____

2. _____

3. _____

4. _____

5. _____

6. _____

7. _____

8. _____

9. _____

10. _____

What are some things coming up soon that you know are going to be difficult for your partner, and why will they be difficult? What are ways you could help support them?

How has money been a resource for you? What have been some positive things you've been able to learn, get, or do because of money?

_____

_____

_____

_____

_____

_____

_____

What were some good things about being raised by your parents or caregivers? Were there some important lessons you learned that proved valuable? Why or why not?

_____

_____

_____

_____

_____

_____

_____

What were some difficult things about being raised by your parents or caregivers? Despite them being hard, did you learn something valuable that you used later in life?

What are some things you're grateful you learned in school? These could be from academic classes, from socializing with others, or from special activities.

{ What are some opportunities you've had in life? Consider your upbringing, education, certain coursework or certifications, resources, finances, experiences, trips, jobs, and so on.

_____

_____

_____

_____

_____

_____

_____

_____

{ Isn't it amazing that you can read (knowing that others struggle with it)? What's the last book (other than this one), story, magazine, or article you read? Did you like it?

_____

_____

_____

_____

_____

_____

_____

_____

When was the last time you felt amazed that you woke up in the morning? That you honestly thought about how incredible it is that you're alive?

What do you most love about where you sleep? Do you sleep on a mattress? Under sheets and a comforter? With a pillow?

List 10 resentments you currently have. They may be toward people, places, institutions, or concepts. Can you let them go? You can't be grateful and resentful at the same time!

1. _____
2. _____
3. _____
4. _____
5. _____
6. _____
7. _____
8. _____
9. _____
10. _____

1. _____
2. _____
3. _____
4. _____
5. _____
6. _____
7. _____
8. _____
9. _____
10. _____

How does your partner show their love for you? What does your partner love about you that you appreciate? How does it make you feel when they show you that they love you just as you are?

When's the last time you belly-laughed or whole body-laughed? Describe the moment in detail. If you can't remember, make an effort to do so soon.

In what ways are you physically safe? Do you live in a safe area? Do you have locks on your door? Other things that protect you?

In what relationships do you most feel emotionally safe? Relationships where you feel comfortable expressing your feelings and knowing that they'll listen to and validate you.

Do you have an item you like to wear for special occasions, such as a watch or piece of jewelry, favorite shoes, or a hat? Why do you like it?

Was there a time that you were unintentionally without a job? How did it feel? Are you grateful for the security a job and paycheck can provide?

_____

_____

_____

_____

_____

_____

_____

_____

_____

Have you ever been homeless? If not, imagine what that would feel like. How would it feel not to know where you were going to sleep?

_____

_____

_____

_____

_____

_____

_____

_____

{ Describe a time when you felt "strong," however you define it, be it physically, mentally, emotionally, and so on. Did something happen to make you feel that way?

_____

_____

_____

_____

_____

_____

_____

{ What does the word "respect" mean to you? How can or do others show respect for you? How can or do you show respect for yourself?

_____

_____

_____

_____

_____

_____

_____

_____

List 10 things you like about yourself because of your relationship with your partner. Are you more open? Inspired to do new things? Have you achieved certain goals?

1. _____

2. _____

3. _____

4. _____

5. _____

6. _____

7. _____

8. _____

9. _____

10. _____

- -

1. _____

2. _____

3. _____

4. _____

5. _____

6. _____

7. _____

8. _____

9. _____

10. _____

Are there ways you could be better at showing your love for your partner? How? If you need help thinking of specific ideas, ask your partner.

{ Have you ever *not* had a cell phone? What would it be like
if you didn't have one today? What do you most appreciate
about having one?

{ When is the last time you experienced pain, either because of
an injury or after recovering from surgery? If you think about
it, did that pain help you enjoy things differently?

When was the last time you were sick? Like *really* sick? How did not feeling well help you appreciate your health once you were recovered?

_____

_____

_____

_____

_____

_____

_____

_____

Think back to your list of resentments on page 123. Identify which resentment has been weighing on you most heavily. How freeing would it be if you gave it up?

_____

_____

_____

_____

_____

_____

_____

_____

What would it feel like if you no longer held grudges? Would you feel lighter? Freer? More mature? What's holding you back from doing this today?

When is the last time you slept in? How did that feel? Were you able to enjoy it, or did you feel guilty and struggle with not *doing* something?

{ Make an effort to see something beautiful today. What was it? Why did you find it beautiful? How was the process of looking for it helpful?

_____

_____

_____

_____

_____

_____

_____

{ Do you like resolutions, or do you find them difficult to stick to? What are some resolutions you have stuck to? What made them easier for you to hold to?

_____

_____

_____

_____

_____

_____

_____

List 10 people or things that you're grateful are no longer in your life. These items could include a job, a relationship, or even a place you lived.

1. _____
2. _____
3. _____
4. _____
5. _____
6. _____
7. _____
8. _____
9. _____
10. _____

1. _____
2. _____
3. _____
4. _____
5. _____
6. _____
7. _____
8. _____
9. _____
10. _____

What experience are you grateful to have shared with your partner? Did it make you closer? Did it make you see them in a new way?

{ What is a resolution or goal you'd like to stick to or achieve in the next six months? How might a gratitude practice help you in sticking to or achieving it?

_____

_____

_____

_____

_____

_____

_____

{ Acceptance of our present can help us make changes. What things are you presently grateful for, and what would you want to change with your resolution?

_____

_____

_____

_____

_____

_____

_____

{ What is a long-term goal you have, such as saving for the
down payment on a home? How might a gratitude practice
help you achieve it?

_____

_____

_____

_____

_____

_____

_____

{ With respect to your long-term goal, what things are you
grateful for presently, such as having a safe place to rent
or stay?

_____

_____

_____

_____

_____

_____

_____

What are areas in your life where you feel the most confident? At your work? When you're advising a friend? When you're cooking a new dish?

What would it be like if you felt that confident in all areas of your life? What could you do to bring that feeling of confidence?

In what areas of your life or with what people do you wish you were more assertive or stood up for yourself more? Why don't you?

_____

_____

_____

_____

_____

_____

_____

_____

While a lot of us can feel guilty being assertive, it's better in the long run. What is an instance where you feel thankful that you were assertive or stood up for yourself or others?

_____

_____

_____

_____

_____

_____

_____

List 10 people or things that you'd like to *currently* give up, ones that make it difficult for you to be grateful. These might be certain ways of thinking, habits, relationships, and so on.

1. _____
2. _____
3. _____
4. _____
5. _____
6. _____
7. _____
8. _____
9. _____
10. _____

1. _____
2. _____
3. _____
4. _____
5. _____
6. _____
7. _____
8. _____
9. _____
10. _____

How is your partner different today than they were when you first met? What are the positive changes? How have you grown closer because of them?

{ What's a modern convenience you have that you take for granted? A dishwasher? A cell phone? How does it make your life better?

_____

_____

_____

_____

_____

_____

_____

_____

{ When's the last time you *had* to rest? Maybe recovering after a surgery, when the power went out, or while on vacation. What was that like for you?

_____

_____

_____

_____

_____

_____

_____

_____

143

{ While resting can be difficult for some of us, it's likely you
learned some important things. What did you discover that
you wouldn't have discovered otherwise?

_____

_____

_____

_____

_____

_____

_____

_____

{ What was it like the last time you had a really fun time out
with a friend or friends? Describe it. What made that particular time so great?

_____

_____

_____

_____

_____

_____

_____

When was the last time you had to wait, for either an answer, results, or a reward? How could you try to make waits more enjoyable or even just more tolerable in the future?

What hobbies and interests do you currently have that you would sincerely miss if you couldn't do them? Would you like to do them more often?

{ How is where you are in life right now different from where you were a year ago? What are the positive changes between then and now?

_____

_____

_____

_____

_____

_____

_____

_____

{ Where would you like to be in life a year from now? What positive changes would you like to implement between now and then? Be specific.

_____

_____

_____

_____

_____

_____

_____

_____

Keep Being Grateful Together _ _ _ _ _

Congratulations! By finishing this journal with your partner, you've begun a valuable and ultimately life-changing practice. Take some time to reflect on your journey with your partner:

1. What did you start doing differently as a result of this gratitude journal? What did you notice your partner doing differently?

2. How do you and your partner practice gratitude? What do you most like about it?

3. How has your overall mood or feeling been since you started a practice of gratitude? Have you noticed a change in your partner?

4. How have things been between you and your partner since you started this practice? Would you consider them better?

5. Have you experienced a tough time personally since beginning this practice? Did you find yourself dealing with it differently than you might have before?

6. Have you and your partner experienced a struggle since beginning this practice? Did you deal with it differently than you would have before?

7. Which of the prompts or lists did you like most? Which ones surprised you? Which ones helped you realize or learn something new about your partner?

8. Take a look back at the Guided Prompts on pages 2 and 3. Redo them with your partner and then compare your responses to the ones that you had originally. Have your answers changed?

As illustrated in countless studies, people benefit the most from gratitude when they make it a part of daily life. You can do this by keeping a gratitude journal or writing gratitude lists. Say "thank you" to anyone who helps you, even if they just hold a door open for you. Do something regularly, like texting at least three people every week how much you appreciate them. When something difficult happens, look for the silver lining, and don't forget that gratitude is best expressed through action.

If you and your partner would like to continue a practice of gratitude together, consider picking a specific time every day to connect this way. If you can't do every day, try once a week. As long as you commit to it together, you'll still see positive benefits. You can pick a random prompt or list from this journal and redo it. You can write a shared gratitude list or share one positive thing you saw that day with each other.

Regardless of how you and your partner choose to keep being grateful together, know that happiness arises from gratitude. Enjoy being happier together.

Resources

***Thanks! How the New Science of Gratitude Can Make You Happier* by Robert Emmons:** This book includes both a summary of research on gratitude and clear and practical ways to begin seeing your life in a more positive way.

***A Simple Act of Gratitude: How Learning to Say Thank You Changed My Life* by John Kralik:** John Kralik's touching memoir shows how even small acts of gratitude can change our lives. It also provides a simple road map for doing it yourself.

***Gratitude* by Oliver Sacks:** A collection of essays originally published in *The New York Times* after Sacks learned of a devastating cancer diagnosis; this book is a must-read.

***Everyday Gratitude* by A Network for Grateful Living:** This book showcases beautiful pictures with quotes on gratitude from influential figures, like Anne Frank. Every quote shows exactly how happiness arises from gratitude.

***Good Days Start with Gratitude: A 52-Week Guide to Cultivate an Attitude of Gratitude: Gratitude Journal* by Pretty Simple Press:** If you'd like to continue the practice of gratitude on your own, this well-designed journal is for you. Fill it out daily for 52 weeks!

"Gratitude and Well-Being: A Review and Theoretical Integration" by Alex M. Wood, Jeffrey J. Froh, and Adam W. A. Geraghty (DOI: 10.1016/j.cpr.2010.03.005): This 2010 study published in *Clinical Psychology Review* reveals how a personal practice of gratitude positively affects a person's social, physical, and emotional well-being and coping skills.

"Expressing Gratitude to a Partner Leads to More Relationship Maintenance Behavior" by Nathaniel M. Lambert and Frank D. Fincham (DOI: 10.1037/a0021557): This 2011 study published in *Emotion* shows that a regular gratitude practice can lead to a positive perception of your partner and thus make it easier to resolve conflicts.

Gratefulness.org: This website offers videos, programs, e-courses, and resources (both community-based and online) for anyone wanting to begin a life-changing practice of gratitude.

Gratitude app: Want to start a daily gratitude journal but hate writing things down? This app gives you a gratitude journal on your phone plus daily affirmations.

Greater Good Science Center (greatergood.Berkeley .edu): A fantastic resource for how to apply cutting-edge science on gratitude toward improving your own well-being as well as to any of your relationships.

ACKNOWLEDGMENTS

Many thanks to the brilliant, delightful team at Callisto Media, including Sean Newcott, Caryn Abramowitz, and many others who all helped make this book what it is. You made writing this easy. I'm also indebted to all of the clients I've worked with throughout the years. Without your trust in me, this book would never have happened. Last, but never least, thank you to my wonderful husband, Brian, who's supported me in everything that I do, and who, when I first told him I hoped to write a book for couples one day, said, "Why wouldn't you?" Writers never write alone, so much thanks also to my dear writing friends: Ashley Shannon, Kerry Kerr McAvoy, Kelly Eden, and anyone else I may have missed.

ABOUT THE AUTHOR

 **Tara Blair Ball** is a Certified Relationship Coach and writer who specializes in helping clients have happy and healthy relationships. She has a bachelor's degree from Rhodes College (2008) and a master's from the University of Memphis (2012), along with coaching certifications from Transformation Academy and courses fully accredited by Complementary Therapists Accredited Association (CTAA). She lives outside Memphis, Tennessee, with her husband, Brian, and their four children. When Ball isn't coaching clients, writing, or filming TikToks, you can find her reading a sci-fi novel. If you want to discover new tools for improving the emotional intimacy and communication in your relationships, find her on Instagram and TikTok at @tara. relationshipcoach or her website at TaraBlairBall.com.

CPSIA information can be obtained
at www.ICGtesting.com
Printed in the USA
LVHW072150091121
702925LV00017B/965